SONGS AND GAMES

An Exciting Collection for Boys and Girls

This 2000 edition is published by Derrydale Books,
an imprint of Random House Value Publishing, Inc.,
280 Park Avenue, New York, New York 10017.

Random House
New York • Toronto • London • Sydney • Auckland
http://www.randomhouse.com/

Printed and bound in Singapore

Library of Congress Cataloging-in-Publication Data
Songs and games / illustrated by Anne Anderson and Margaret W. Tarrant.
1 score.
Children's songs and singing games, with piano acc.
1. Children's songs. 2. Singing games. [1. Songs. 2. Singing games. 3. Games.]
I. Anderson, Anne, ill. II. Tarrant, Margaret W., 1888–1959, ill.
M1992.S69 1994
94-17196
CIP
M AC

ISBN: 0-517-10191-2

8 7 6 5 4 3 2

Songs and Games

An Exciting Collection
for Boys and Girls

DERRYDALE BOOKS
NEW YORK

Contents

Introduction

A child's love of singing songs and playing games awakens with the very first lullaby and peekaboo. An early Pat a Cake elicits a glowing toothless grin, and Musical Chairs thrills even the youngest scrambling player. In this lovely book, with illustrations by Anne Anderson and Margaret W. Tarrant, there are more than fifty songs and games that will entertain girls and boys of all ages.

Children are always ready to sing, and these classic songs are as charming today as they were when your great-grandparents were children. Since the world of a child is filled with magic and enchantment, it's no surprise that the baked birds in Sing a Song of Sixpence can burst into song, or that Little Bo-Peep's sheep can lose their tails. In a world of mystery and wonder, Twinkle, Twinkle, Little Star has real meaning. And life can be just plain silly, too, so why shouldn't a cow jump over the moon? From a child's perspective these old rhymes are fresh and new.

Parties and get-togethers for the smallest set should be short and simple. Plan your party from the Songs section of this book: a couple of songs—perhaps with rhythm instruments and a parade—and light refreshments are all you need. Older children who can be organized into a line or a circle and can follow simple directions are ready for more structured group play.

In the Games section you'll find many of the tried-and-true

favorites from your own childhood, along with a wonderful selection of older games adapted for modern children. Included are action games, guessing games, and games of skill.

As you plan the games, keep the ages of your young guests in mind. For the youngest children try simpler games, like Musical Chairs, The Mulberry Bush, and Heading the Balloon.

Good guessing games are a hit with all ages. In "Who Spoke," a blindfolded child must recognize another player's voice; in "Tip It!" one team hides a penny from another; and in Find the Thimble, children search for a thimble hidden in plain sight—and it's surprisingly challenging!

Children love to answer riddles. In "I've Got a Little Basket," they go through the alphabet naming items in their "basket"; in Advertisements, they must think of brand-name products. Finally, children enjoy singing and action—and many of the games in this book give them the opportunity to rhyme, and sing, and run around in circles chasing their friends.

As for the oldest children, don't let them convince you that they are "too old" to play games. These children particularly enjoy the action of the Racing Game, and love the challenge of a guessing game like Character Sketching, or a number game like Buzz Fizz.

You don't have to wait for a special occasion to treat children to songs and games. Whether riding in the car, playing with a friend, or nestling into bed, little ones will delight in a sing-along. And anytime you have a group of children gathered in your home, before they can chant the age-old refrain "There's nothing to do," you can open this book and, with no expense or special equipment, turn an ordinary afternoon into a memorable party.

NINA ROSENSTEIN

SONGS

Hey Diddle Diddle

Hey! did - dle did - dle, the cat and the fid - dle, The

cow jump'd o-ver the moon. The lit-tle dog laugh'd to see such sport, And the

dish ran af-ter the spoon. And the dish ran af-ter the spoon.

Humpty Dumpty

Hump-ty Dump-ty sat on a wall,

Hump-ty Dump-ty had a great fall; All the King's hor-ses and

all the King's men Could-n't put Hump-ty to-ge-ther a-gain.

Little Bo-Peep

1. Lit-tle Bo-peep Has lost her sheep, And does-n't know where to find them: Leave them a-lone, And they'll come home, And bring their tails be-hind them.

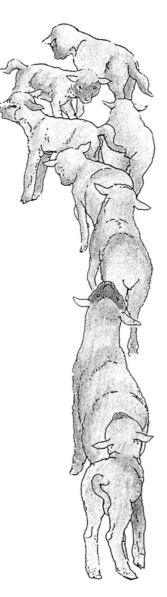

2.
  Little Bo-peep
  Fell fast asleep,
And dreamt she heard them bleating;
  But when she awoke,
  She found it a joke,
For still they all were fleeing.

3.
  Then up she took
  Her little crook,
Determined for to find them
  She found them indeed
  But it made her heart bleed,
For they left their tails behind them.

4
  It happened one day,
  As Bo-peep did stray
Unto a meadow nearby,
  There she spied
  Their tails side by side,
All hung on a tree to dry.

Old King Cole

Old King Cole was a mer-ry old__ soul, And a

mer-ry old soul was he, And he call'd for his pipe and he

call'd for his bowl, And he call'd for his fid-dlers three. Now

Sing a Song of Sixpence

1. Sing a song of six - pence, a pock - et full of rye,

Four and twen - ty black - birds baked__ in a pie;

When the pie was o - pen'd the birds be - gan to sing,

Was-n't that a dain-ty dish to set be-fore a king?

2.
The King was in his counting house,
  counting out his money,
The Queen was in the parlor,
  eating bread and honey,

3.
The maid was in the garden,
  hanging out the clothes,
There came a little blackbird,
  and snapped at her nose.

Rub - a - dub, dub, Three men in a tub,

Who do you think they were?__ The but - cher, the ba - ker, The

can - dle - stick ma-ker, And they are all gone to the fair.__

See-Saw, Marjory Daw

See - saw, Mar-jo-ry Daw,

Har - ry shall have a new mas-ter; He shall have but a

pen-ny a day, Be-cause he won't work an-y fast - er.

Jack and Jill

1. Jack and Jill went up the hill To fetch a pail of wa-ter; Jack fell down and

broke his crown, And Jill came tumb-ling af - ter.

2.
Then up Jack got and home did trot,
  As fast as he could caper;
Dame Jill had the job to plaster his nob
  With vinegar and brown paper.

3.
Jill came in, and she did grin
  To see his paper plaster;
Her mother, vexed, did spank her next
  For laughing at Jack's disaster.

4.
This made Jill pout, and she ran out,
  And Jack did quickly follow;
They rode dog Ball, till Jill did fall,
  Which made Jack laugh and holler.

Three Blind Mice

Three blind mice,

Three blind mice,

See how they run!

See how they run! They

all ran af - ter the farm - er's wife, Who

cut off their tails with a carv - ing knife, Did you

ev - er see such a thing in your life, as

Three blind mice.

Mistress Mary

Mis-tress Ma - ry, quite con-tra - ry,

How does your gar - den grow?__ With sil - ver bells and

coc-kle shells, And pret-ty maids all in a row.__

Simple Simon

1. Sim - ple Si - mon   met   a pie-man

Go - ing to the   fair.   Says Sim - ple Si - mon

to   the pie - man: "Let   me taste   your   ware."

2.
Says the pieman to Simple Simon:
  "Show me first your penny."
Says Simple Simon to the pieman:
  "Indeed I have not any."

3.
Simple Simon went a-fishing
  For to catch a whale,
But all the water he had got
  Was in his mother's pail.

4.
Simple Simon went to look
  If plums grew on a thistle.
He pricked his finger very much
  Which made poor Simon whistle.

Little Jack Horner

Lit-tle Jack Hor-ner sat in a cor-ner,

Eat-ing a Christ-mas pie;__ He put in his thumb, and

pull'd out a plum, And said, "What a good boy am I!"

Ride a Cock Horse

Ride a cock horse to Ban - bur - y Cross, To

see a fine la - dy up - on a white horse;

Rings on her fin - gers and bells on her toes,

She shall have mu - sic wher - ev - er she goes.

Twinkle, Twinkle, Little Star

1. Twin-kle, twin-kle, lit-tle star, How I

won-der what you are, Up a-bove the world so

high, Like a dia-mond in the sky. Twin-kle,

twin-kle, lit - tle star, How I won-der what you are.

2.

When the blazing sun is gone,
When it nothing shines upon,
Then you show your little light,
Twinkle, twinkle all the night.
  Twinkle, twinkle little star,
  How I wonder what you are.

3.

Then the traveler in the dark
Thanks you for your tiny spark.
Could he see which way to go
If you did not twinkle so?
  Twinkle, twinkle little star,
  How I wonder what you are.

4.

In the dark blue sky you keep,
While you through my curtains peep,
And you never shut your eye
Till the sun is in the sky.
  Twinkle, twinkle little star,
  How I wonder what you are.

Tom, Tom, the Piper's Son

Tom, Tom, the Pi - per's son,

Stole a pig and a - way did run; The pig was eat and

Tom was beat, Which sent him howl - ing down the street.

Baa Baa Black Sheep

Baa, baa, black sheep, have you an - y wool?

Yes, sir, yes, sir, three bags full. One for the mas - ter,

one for the dame, And one for the lit - tle boy that lives in our lane.

What Are Little Boys Made of?

1. What are lit-tle boys made of?

What are lit-tle boys made of? Frogs and snails and

pup-py dog's tails, That's what lit-tle boys are made of.

2.
What are little girls made of?
What are little girls made of?
Sugar and spice, and everything nice.
That's what little girls are made of.

3.
What are young men made of?
What are young men made of?
Sighs and leers and crocodile tears,
That is what young men are made of.

4.
What are young women made of?
What are young women made of?
Ribbons and laces, and sweet pretty faces,
That is what young women are made of.

Pussy Cat, Pussy Cat

Pus - sy cat, pus - sy cat, where have you been?

I've been to Lon-don to look at the Queen. Pus-sy cat, pus-sy cat,

what did you there? I caught a lit-tle mouse un-der her chair.

Curly Locks

1. Cur - ly locks! cur - ly locks!
2. sit on a cush - ion And

Wilt thou be mine?__ Thou shalt not wash
sew a fine seam,__ And feed up - on

dish - es, Nor yet feed the swine, But
straw - ber - ries, Su - gar and cream.

Hickory Dickory Dock

Hick-o-ry, dick-o-ry, dock! __ The mouse ran up__ the clock,__ The clock struck one, And down it ran, Hick - o-ry, dick - o - ry, dock!__

2.
Hickory, dickory, dock,
The mouse ran up the clock,
The clock struck three,
The mouse ran away,
Hickory, dickory, dock.

3.
Hickory, dickory, dock,
The mouse ran up the clock,
The clock struck ten,
The mouse came again,
Hickory, dickory, dock.

Girls and Boys, Come Out to Play

Girls and boys, come out to play, The moon doth shine as

bright as day; Leave your sup - per and leave your sleep, And

join your play-fel - lows in the street. Come with a whoop!

Come with a call! Come with a good will or not at all.

Up the lad-der and down the wall, A half-pen-ny roll will serve us all.

You find milk, and I'll find flour, And we'll have a pud-ding in half an hour.

I Saw Three Ships

1. I saw three ships come sail - ing by,

Sail - ing by, sail - ing by, I saw three ships come

sail - ing by, On New Year's Day in the morn - ing.

2.
And what do you think was in them then?
   In them then?
   In them then?
And what do you think was in them then,
   On New Year's Day in the morning.

3.
Three pretty girls were in them then,
   In them then,
   In them then,
Three pretty girls were in them then,
   On New Year's Day in the morning.

4.
And one could whistle, one could sing,
   The other played on the violin,
Such joy there was at my wedding,
   On New Year's Day in the morning.

Baby Baby Bunting

Ba - by ba - by Bunt - ing,

Dad - dy's gone a hunt - ing; Gone to get a

rab - bit skin, To wrap the ba - by Bunt - ing in.

Pat a Cake, Pat a Cake, Baker's Man

Pat a cake, pat a cake, ba-ker's man,
Please make me a cake, as fast as you can.
Pat it and prick it and mark it with B,
And put it in th'ov-en for Ba-by and me.

Ding Dong Bell

Ding, dong, bell! Pus - sy's in the well.

Who put her in? Lit - tle Tom-my Thin. Who pull'd her out?

Lit - tle Tom - my Stout. What a naught - y boy was that, To

Sleep, Baby, Sleep

1. Sleep, ba - by, sleep! Thy fa - ther wat-ches the sheep, And tend - eth the lambs up - on yon - der hill, But

mo - ther wat-ches one dear-er still, Sleep, ba - by, sleep.___

2.

   Sleep, baby, sleep!

   Soft be thy slumbers and deep,

While over our heads wild winds meet.

An old, old lullaby they repeat:

   Sleep, baby, sleep!

3.

   Sleep, baby, sleep!

   Thy father watches the sheep,

And tendeth the lambs upon yonder hill,

But mother watches one dearer still,

   Sleep, baby, sleep!

Hush-a-Bye Baby

Hush-a-bye, ba - by, On the tree top,

When the wind blows the cradle will rock, when the bough breaks The

cra-dle will fall: Down will come cra-dle And ba-by and all.

GAMES WITH SONGS

London Bridge Is Falling Down

This age-old favorite continues to delight children. Two players are chosen to make the bridge. They raise their arms and join hands and the other players march around under the bridge. Everyone sings the song. At the last verse, the player who is passing beneath the bridge is made a prisoner, and must choose to stand behind one of the players forming the bridge. When all the players have been made prisoners, a tug-of-war completes the game.

1. Lon - don Bridge is fall-ing down,

Fall-ing down, fall-ing down, Lon - don Bridge is

fall - ing down, My fair la - dy.___

2.
How shall we build it up again?
Up again, up again,
How shall we build it up again,
   My fair lady?

3.
Build it up with silver and gold,
Silver and gold, silver and gold,
Build it up with silver and gold,
   My fair lady.

4.
Silver and gold will be stolen away,
Stolen away, stolen away,
Silver and gold will be stolen away,
   My fair lady.

5.
Build it up with iron and steel,
Iron and steel, iron and steel,
Build it up with iron and steel,
   My fair lady.

6.
Iron and steel will rust and break,
Rust and break, rust and break,
Iron and steel will rust and break,
   My fair lady.

7.
Build it up with wood and clay,
Wood and clay, wood and clay,
Build it up with wood and clay,
   My fair lady.

8.
Wood and clay will wash away,
Wash away, wash away,
Wood and clay will wash away,
   My fair lady.

9.
Build it up with stone so strong,
Stone so strong, stone so strong,
It will last for ages long,
   My fair lady.

10.
Here's a prisoner we have caught,
We have caught, we have caught,
Here's a prisoner we have caught,
   My fair lady.

The Mulberry Bush

All the players form a circle and act out the following song. During the chorus, which is repeated after each verse, the players join hands and dance around.

Here we go round the mul-ber-ry bush, The

mul - ber-ry bush, The mul - ber-ry bush, Here we go round the

mul - ber-ry bush, So ear - ly in the morn - ing.

Chorus

Here we go round the mulberry bush,
    the mulberry bush,
    the mulberry bush,
Here we go round the mulberry bush
    so early in the morning.

1.

This is the way we clap our hands.

2.

This is the way we brush our shoes.

3.

This is the way we wash our hands.

4.

This is the way we wash our faces.

5.

This is the way we brush our hair.

6.

This is the way we brush our clothes.

7.

This is the way we work at school.

8.

This is the way we run from school.

Nuts in May

The players take sides, and face each other in two rows. The players on the first side join hands and step forward and back, while singing the verse to the tune of "The Mulberry Bush."

The players on the other side then join hands and step forward and back while singing the next verse. Where the song lyrics say "Charlie" or "Rosie," players should name one player from each row. The sides then continue alternately until the end of the song.

Then the two players who have been named meet at the center line. With their right feet touching, and holding each other by their right hands, they have a tug-of-war. The child pulled over the line then joins the side of the other.

The game is repeated, but the first line is now sung by the side that previously sang the second line.

The game continues in this way until all the players are on one side.

1.

Here we go gathering nuts in May,
    Nuts in May, nuts in May.
Here we go gathering nuts in May,
    At six o'clock in the morning.

2.

And whom will we gather for nuts in May?
    Nuts in May, nuts in May.
And Whom shall we gather for nuts in May,
    At six o'clock in the morning.

3.

We'll gather "Charlie" for nuts in May,
    Nuts in May, nuts in May.
We'll gather "Charlie" for nuts in May,
    At six o'clock in the morning.

4.

Whom shall we send to take him away?
    Take him away, take him away.
Whom shall we send to take him away,
    At six o'clock in the morning.

5.

We'll send "Rosie" to take him away,
    Take him away, take him away.
We'll send "Rosie" to take him away,
    At six o'clock in the morning.

Oranges and Lemons

Two of the taller players hold each other's hands and raise their arms to form an archway. One of these players is named "Orange," and the other "Lemon," but their names are kept secret from the others. The singing begins, and the players follow one another around and around under the arch. At the final "ding dong" the arch falls and encloses the player who happens to be underneath. The prisoner is then asked in a whisper whether he or she will have Orange or Lemon, and according to his or her choice, which should also be made in a whisper, the prisoner is sent to stand behind either Orange or Lemon.

The game then continues, and another player is caught in the same way. The game goes on until all the players are standing behind either Orange or Lemon. Then the players prepare for a tug-of-war by putting their hands around the waist of the person in front of them. Orange and Lemon then join hands and pull; the stronger side is the winner.

Incidentally, Saint Clement's, Saint Martin's, and all the other places named in the song are London churches, and when their bells ring, they sound as if they are saying the words that are quoted.

1. O-ran-ges and le-mons! say the bells of Saint Cle-ment's. You

owe me five far-things, say the bells of Saint Mar-tin's. When will you pay me? say the

bells of Old Bai-ley   When I grow rich say the bells of Shore-ditch.

Ding dong ding ding dong, Ding   dong ding ding dong.

2.
"When will that be?" say the bells of Stepney.
"I do not know," says the great bell of Bow.
"Pancakes and fritters," say the bells of Saint Peter's.
"Two sticks and an apple," say the bells of Whitechapel.
    Ding dong, ding ding dong,
    Ding dong, ding ding dong.

3.
"Old father Bald-pate," say the slow bells of Aldgate.
"Pokers and tongs," say the bells of Saint John's.
"Kettles and pans," say the bells of Saint Anne's.
"Brickbats and tiles," say the bells of Saint Giles.
    Ding dong, ding ding dong,
    Ding dong, ding ding dong.

GAMES

Musical Instruments

The players sit in a semicircle. Each one chooses a musical instrument, other than the piano, which he or she will pretend to play. One player is chosen to be the conductor, and sits in front of the group, pretending to play the piano. The conductor then begins to imitate any other instrument that is being represented, and as soon as he or she does so, the player of that instrument must pretend to play the piano. When the conductor moves on to another instrument, this player must return to playing his or her original instrument. During the game the players sing the first verse of "Twinkle, Twinkle, Little Star," and the conductor continues to "trade" instruments with the other players.

The game continues until the conductor sees a player who has not begun "playing the piano" when his or her instrument is imitated. That player becomes the conductor, and the game starts over with everyone, except the new conductor, choosing a different instrument.

"Who Spoke?"
A Whispering Game

The players stand close together in a circle. One player is blind-folded and stands in the center.

The players in the circle join hands and sing a short song, perhaps the first verse of "London Bridge Is Falling Down," while moving around the circle. At the conclusion of the singing, the blindfolded player in the center points toward the ring and whis-pers, "Who is there?" The player pointed at must then whisper, "It's me," trying to disguise his or her voice as much as possible. This little conversation may be repeated no more than three times, after which the player in the center must try to name the person being pointed at.

If the guess is correct, they exchange places. If the guess is not correct, the singing begins again and the game continues.

During the whispering it is important that all the other players be completely quiet.

Advertisements

All the players sit in a circle except the leader, who stands in the center. The leader is given a handkerchief, which he or she throws at one of the seated players and then begins counting to ten as quickly as possible.

Each seated player should be thinking of the name of some product, like Birds Eye frozen peas, Hershey's chocolate syrup, Pepperidge Farm bread, or Thomas' English muffins. When the handkerchief is thrown at a player he or she must answer with a product's name. The same product may not be named more than once. A player who repeats an answer, or who does not answer before the counting is finished, exchanges places with the leader.

Earth, Air, Fire, and Water

All the players sit in a circle except the leader, who stands in the center. The leader is given a handkerchief, which he or she throws at one of the seated players, calling out at the same time either earth, air, fire, or water.

If the leader says "Earth," the seated player must answer with the name of an animal that walks upon the earth. If the leader says "Air," then the player must answer with the name of a bird. And if the leader says "Water," the player must reply with the name of a fish. If the leader says "Fire," the seated player must get up, turn around, and sit down.

The answer or the action must be completed before the leader can count to ten. If this is not done, the two players exchange places, and the game continues.

One Finger, One Thumb

Everyone sits in a semicircle. Until this game is thoroughly learned, it is best for one person to sit in front of the group, chant each verse, and perform the movements for everyone to copy.

When chanting the first verse, the players move the first finger and thumb of the right hand. Then for the next verse the two first fingers and two thumbs are moved. The game continues with the actions suiting the words. The actions are always performed first on the right side and then on the left.

When everyone knows the game, a race through it without stopping is a great deal of fun.

1.

One finger, one thumb,
Get up, turn around,
Sit down. Hurray! Hurray!

2.

Two fingers, two thumbs,
Get up, turn around,
Sit down. Hurray! Hurray!

3.

Two fingers, two thumbs, one arm,
Get up, turn around,
Sit down. Hurray! Hurray!

4.

Two fingers, two thumbs, two arms,
Get up, turn around,
Sit down. Hurray! Hurray!

5.

Two fingers, two thumbs,
Two arms, one leg,
Get up, turn around,
Sit down. Hurray! Hurray!

6.

Two fingers, two thumbs,
Two arms, two legs,
Get up, turn around,
Sit down. Hurray! Hurray!

7.

Two fingers, two thumbs,
Two arms, two legs, one head,
Get up, turn around,
Sit down. Hurray! Hurray!

"My Light Shines!"

Two players leave the room and choose two homonyms—words that sound the same but have different meanings, like hare and hair, pear and pair, palm (tree) and palm (of the hand). Proper names may not be used.

The players return to the room and begin to give hints about the words they have chosen to be. They may even give clues about each other, as long as it is clear which player's word is being described. They should not, of course, describe themselves so well that the other players can guess too easily.

A player who thinks that he or she has guessed either or both of the words must not call out the answers, but instead says, "My light shines!" and then asks subtle questions about the words. If it is obvious by these questions that the player is wrong, he or she is quickly told that the "light" has "gone out." The game goes on until all or most of the players have guessed the two words.

Gossip

This popular and amusing game, also known as Telephone, shows how gossip can change a story.

All the players sit in a ring. The one chosen to begin whispers a sentence of any kind, only once, into the next player's ear. That player whispers what he or she thinks was said into the next player's ear.

The sentence is then whispered to each player in turn until the last player is reached. This player then says aloud what he or she has heard, and so, going backward around the circle, does each player. The twisting and turning of the words causes great amusement.

Another player then starts with another sentence and the game starts again.

Filling the Gap

The players form a circle, joining hands. One player is chosen to run around the outside of the circle and touch another player. That player then starts to run in the opposite direction. The two players try to reach the vacant place first. The one who does not "fill the gap" continues to run around the circle, and then touches another player. The game continues in this way.

Passing the Pennies

The players are seated in two straight lines facing each other. Extra chairs are placed at both ends of each line. At one end of each line, six pennies are placed on the extra chair.

At a given signal, the players seated next to the end chairs take a penny and hand it to their neighbors, who pass it to the next person. In this way a penny is passed as quickly as possible down each line, until it is placed on the empty chair at the other end, where it must remain.

As soon as the first penny has reached the end chair, a second penny is passed down the line, and so on, until all the pennies have been placed upon the far chairs. Then they are immediately passed back, one by one, in the opposite direction. The side that first returns them to their original place wins the game.

The pennies may only be passed with the right hand, and every player must have a turn. Should a player drop a penny, he or she must find it before passing any more pennies. A referee should be chosen, who carefully watches to be sure that no rules are broken.

Character Sketching

An uneven number of players is necessary for this game.

The players are seated in two equal lines facing each other. Another player takes a seat at one end, and begins to give a description of a well-known person—either a public figure, a movie star, or someone, perhaps a teacher, who is known to all the players. It may even be one of the other players.

As soon as a player guesses who is being described, he or she must call out the name of that person. If the answer is correct, all the players, including the one who gave the description, get up and run to get seats on the opposite row. The player who is left standing then becomes the speaker and describes another character.

The briefer and clearer the description, the greater the fun.

Ten Tongue Twisters

One old ox opening oysters.

Two toads, totally tired, trying to trot to Tutbury.

Three tigers, taking tea.

Four fishermen, fishing for frogs.

Five fantastic Frenchmen, fanning five fainting fleas.

Six sensible sailors, selling soup.

Seven southern salmon.

Eight enthusiastic Englishmen, earnestly examining Europe.

Nine ninepenny ninepins.

Ten tinning tanning tonies, tanning tinder for tea.

The players sit in a circle. The player chosen to go first has a copy of the ten tongue twisters and says the first line to his or her neighbor, who then repeats it to the next player, and so on, until all the players have said it in turn.

The first player then says the second line, followed by the first. These two lines are repeated by all the players in turn. The third line is then said, followed by the second and then the first. The game continues until each player has tried to say all ten lines, beginning with the last and continuing backward to the first.

"Tip It!"

Two teams are formed and a captain is chosen for each one. The players sit at a table, each team facing the other. Each captain sits in the center of his or her team. The players on one team put their hands under the table and pass a nickel from hand to hand, trying not to let the players on the other team know where it is.

The captain of the other team then says, "Hands up!" and everyone on the team with the nickel must put their hands, closed into fists, on the table. The captain then says, "Hands down!" and they must put their hands, palms down, on the table. As much noise as possible should be made with their hands so the coin will not be heard as it hits the table.

The first member of the opposing team then tries to guess who has the nickel. The person doing the guessing says, "Hands off the table!" to anyone he or she thinks does not have the nickel, and says "Tip it!" to the player suspected of having the nickel. If the nickel is discovered, the guessing team wins a point. If the nickel is not discovered, the hiding team gets the point. The nickel is then given to the other team, and the game continues in the same way. The players on either side guess in turn. The first team to get ten points is the winner.

Blind Man's Bluff

This game has certainly withstood the test of time. It is as much fun today as it was in Grandma and Grandpa's day.

One player is blindfolded and then does his or her best to tag one of the other players, all of whom must try to avoid being tagged. When someone is finally caught, the blindfolded player must try to guess who it is by feeling the hair, face, and clothes. If he or she does not succeed after three guesses, the blindfold remains in place and the game continues. If the blindfolded player guesses correctly, however, the captured player must take his or her place.

"I've Got a Little Basket"

This is one of many alphabet games.

One player says, "I've got a little basket." The player on his or her left asks, "And what have you in it?" The first player replies, "Something beginning with *A*." The second player must then name something beginning with *A*, for example, "Apples." This player then says to the player on his or her left, "I have a little basket," and when asked, "What have you in it?" answers, "Something beginning with *B*."

The game continues this way until the players have gone through all the letters of the alphabet.

Memory Game

Each player is given paper and a pencil. A collection of many miscellaneous articles, the more varied the better, is brought in on a covered tray. The tray is uncovered and the players then look at them for a short time. (The length of time should be decided before the game begins, according to the number of articles on the tray.) The tray is covered again. The players then make a list of all the things they remember seeing on the tray. When the time is up, the tray is uncovered and the lists corrected. Each correct article on a list scores a point. Anyone naming an incorrect article loses a point. The player who gets the greatest number of points is the winner.

Cat and Mouse

The players make a circle and join hands. One player, who has been chosen to be the Cat, stands outside the circle. Another player, who has been selected to be the Mouse, stays within the ring. Upon the signal "Go!" the Cat tries to catch the Mouse, following as he or she runs in and out of the circle, beneath the joined hands of the other players.

The players forming the circle give the Mouse every opportunity of leaving and entering by raising their arms, while they try to keep the Cat away from the Mouse by lowering their arms. When the Mouse is touched by the Cat, the last two players to allow the Cat to pass must then become Cat and Mouse.

Card-Throwing Game

A pot or bowl is placed on the floor at one end of the room. A chair is placed about nine feet away from it. The player chosen to go first sits on the chair and is given ten ordinary playing cards. The player must throw the cards, one by one, into the pot or bowl.

The chair must remain firmly on the ground, but the player may sit as close to the edge and may stretch as far forward as he or she pleases. The player may not, however, rise from the seat.

For each card thrown into the pot or bowl, without breaking any of the rules, the player gets one point. After all the players have had turns at throwing the cards, the one with the highest score is the winner.

I Sent a Letter to My Love

The players make a circle and join hands. One player, holding a handkerchief, walks around the outside of the circle while reciting the following poem:

I sent a letter to my love,
    and on the way I dropped it;
But one of you has picked it up,
    and put it in a pocket,
Not you, not you,
    not you, not you. . .

This done, the player continues with "Not you, not you, not you, not you." Each time "Not you" is said, he or she taps one player, until, finishing with "But you," he or she drops the handkerchief and begins to run around the outside of the circle. The player who has been selected must pick up the handkerchief and run in the opposite direction, with both players trying to reach the vacant place. The player who reaches the place last takes the handkerchief and continues the game.

Find the Ring

The players sit in a circle and hold a circle of string, to which a small brass ring has been attached. The string must not be too loose, and the players must not sit too far apart. The string, with the ring, is then kept moving around the circle of players from hand to hand.

One player stands in the center of the circle and tries to locate the moving ring. To distract the searcher's attention, the players must say things about the movements of the ring, or sing, "The ring it is moving, I don't know where," or "The ring it is coming, Hurray! Hurray!!"

When the searcher touches a player's hand, the player must open it and show whether he or she is holding the ring. When the search is successful, the player who was holding the ring must switch places with the player in the center.

Racing Game

This relay race should be played outdoors or in a large playroom.

The players are divided into two teams. They line up facing a wall that is a good distance away.

The player at the head of each team is given an object like a small ball, a stone, or, perhaps, a jack to hold. At a given signal, each of the leading players must run to the wall and back, giving the object to the second player on his or her team. This is repeated by each player, until it is the turn of the last player, who runs to the wall and, returning, must place the object in a basket provided for the purpose. The winning team is the one whose object is placed first in the basket.

A Sailor from Botany Bay

One player is chosen to be the old sailor. He hobbles into the circle made by the other players. He then questions each player in turn as much as he wishes, beginning the conversation with:

"Here comes an old sailor from Botany Bay,

And what have you got to give him today?"

When the player answers he or she must always say, "Pork and greens." If the player laughs, he or she is out. It will be difficult not to laugh if the sailor asks such questions as "Who made your coat?" or "What color is your hair?"

The success of this game depends upon the skill of the sailor.

Three Blind Mice

The point of this game is to substitute actions for words wher-ever possible. One player acts as leader, and the others copy whatever he or she does.

1st Round—Hold up three fingers, shut your eyes, say "Mice."

2nd Round—Hold up three fingers, shut your eyes, say "Mice." Open your eyes wide, say "how they," then make a motion of running, with your hands.

3rd Round—Repeat first two rounds. Then:

   Say "They all," make a motion as before with your hands, finishing up with an extra dash to indicate *after*, then say "the farmer's wife."

4th Round—Repeat first three lines, continue by saying:

   "She," then make a motion of cutting off a tail, and say "their tails with a carving knife."

5th Round—As before, and then:

   Say "Did you ever," open your eyes wide and say "such a thing in your life as," hold up three fingers, shut your eyes, and say "mice."

Heading the Balloon

A rope is stretched across the room about level with the height of the shortest player. The players are divided into two teams, each on one side of the rope.

The players toss a balloon over the rope from side to side by touching it only with their heads. If the balloon is pushed under instead of over the rope, or someone touches it with his or her hand, a point is scored by the other team. The side that scores a stated number of points, perhaps six, is declared the winner.

The Fox and the Geese

One of the players acts the part of the Fox. The others are the Geese and stand in a line behind one another, with their hands on each other's shoulders. The player at the front of the line is the Mother Goose, or the Father Goose, and has to protect the others with widespread arms from the Fox.

As the Fox tries to get around to touch one of the Geese, the Mother or Father Goose tries to keep the Fox in front. The Geese in the line move with the Mother or Father Goose, staying behind her or him.

When one of the Geese is caught, he or she becomes the Fox, and the Fox then becomes the Mother or Father Goose.

Find the Thimble

For this game all the players leave the room while one person "hides" a thimble where it can be seen. The other players are called in and begin to search for the thimble. When a player sees the thimble he or she sits down, but says nothing. The game continues until everyone has seen the thimble.

The greatest fun is for those players who have found the thimble to watch the efforts of the others.

Remember that the thimble may be put anywhere, but must be placed where it can be seen. Sometimes the most open of places will cause a great deal of searching.

Musical Chairs

This game has been loved by generation after generation of children. Since it is a highly competitive game, you may wish to adapt it for very small children.

A line of chairs, alternately facing in opposite directions, is placed down the center of the room. There should be one chair less than the number of players, who stand ready to walk around the chairs.

An adult plays the piano, or turns on the radio, and the players march around, but must not touch the chairs.

When the music suddenly stops, all the players try to sit down. One player is, of course, left standing, and is out of the game.

A chair at one end of the line is then removed and the game continues. In this way the number of players and the number of chairs are reduced, until, finally, two players are left to run around one chair, which they must not touch. The player who manages to sit when the music stops is the winner.

For a noncompetitive version, just leave all the chairs in place (preschoolers will still have fun), or eliminate chairs, but not children (let them all pile up on the remaining chairs).

Buzz Fizz

This is a number game. The players sit in a circle and the counting is done by each player in turn.

The first says "one," the next, "two," the third, "three," and so on.

Whenever "seven" occurs, however, the player whose turn it is must say "Buzz!" instead. This also applies to any number that includes a seven or multiples of seven. Thus, instead of saying "seventeen," "twenty-eight," or "seventy-two," the player would say "Buzz!" For seventy-seven he must say "Buzz-Buzz!"

This game may be made more difficult, as well as more amusing, when, in addition to the "Buzz!" players must say "Fizz!" whenever a five or a multiple of five occurs.

If a player makes a mistake, he or she is out, and the counting begins again at one. The game continues until the last player becomes the winner.